COLD BREW COFFEE

COLD BREW COFFEE

TECHNIQUES, RECIPES & COCKTAILS

— FOR —

COFFEE'S HOTTEST TREND

CHLOË CALLOW

ILLUSTRATED BY EMMA DIBBEN

MITCHELL BEAZLEY

CONTENTS

INTRODUCTION

So, cold brew coffee. It's considered by some to be the ultimate hipster accessory – flannel shirt, check; beard, check; tattoos, check; obscure, retro hobby, fixie bike, drummer in an indie band, check, check, check; swigging from a bottle of cold brew, super check. Cold brew is part of the world of speciality coffee and all it encompasses: lustworthy, high-tech machines, slow brewing, a geeky focus on quality and precision, instagrammable café interiors and latte art. Viewed as such, coffee, and all it encompasses, could be seen as simply an extension of a bigger lifestyle picture, with cold brew just the most recently spawned trend.

But if you scratch beneath the surface, is there more to the trend than this purely superficial attempt to sell that cool, "creative" freelance lifestyle?

It can't possibly have escaped your attention; cold brew is the current buzzword in coffee shops, cafés, restaurants and bars. Where the cool kids once ordered a flat white, then moved on to brewed pour-over-style coffee, they're now ordering something a good few degrees more chill.

You may not be 100% positive quite what cold brew is, and yet don't want to be *that* person ordering an iced latte when vogue demands that you should totally have gone for a cold drip. We get you. We've got your back here.

We're here to explore the hottest trend for you, get to the very heart of cold brew coffee and give you all the tools that you need to truly master and embrace it for yourself.

That's right, by the time we've finished with you, you'll not only have got your head around the terminology but you'll be buying coffee beans like a pro, making batches of your chosen cold brew religiously and you'll know your immersion brew from your cold brew Negroni and everything in between.

Now roll those flannel shirt sleeves up and let's get involved.

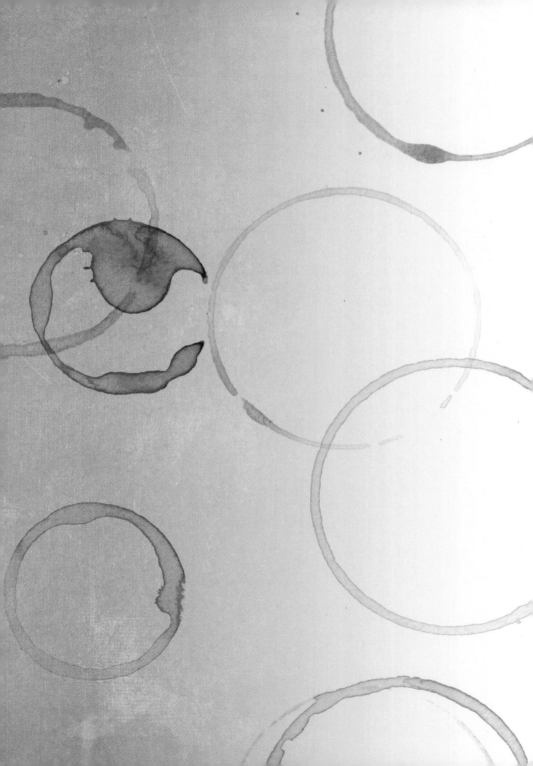

WHY COLD BREW?

You're probably familiar with the general concept of cold brew coffee even if you don't have a full understanding of the whys or how-tos. Well, now's the time to become fully acquainted with this coffee brewing method, which is the latest hot trend and growing fast.

Mysterious jars of brown, chilled liquid now fill entire walls of your local coffee shop, omnipresent and darkly tempting. You may have noticed the bottles lined up in the refrigerator of the trendy neighbourhood restaurant, and you'll definitely have started to see it infiltrating the supermarkets; little cartons and bottles popping up conspicuously on the chiller shelves.

In this book we're going to give you the tools and expertise to keep more than a couple of steps ahead of the zeitgeist. Besides learning how to make your own cold brew, you'll gather tips and enough know-how to be able to adapt your own recipes, not only to create the raw product but also to make cocktails, mocktails and interesting twists on familiar food recipes.

Cold brew coffee can be an acquired taste for the uninitiated, but before you baulk at the idea of a cold, caffeinated beverage, have you thought about the many potential applications for it?

It's not only for sipping on a balmy summer day – though, just for a minute, imagine the thirst-quenching properties of a frosty glass of coffee over ice, pimped up with perhaps a curl of lemon zest, beads of condensation running down the glass... No? Once you've mastered the basics, you'll become proficient in all of its properties, and will be tweaking your brewing recipes and pairing subtle flavours with the flourish of a professional mixologist.

With a bottle in your refrigerator, think of the speed at which you can conjure your morning brew by simply topping it up with hot water. Or use the inherent flavours of different single-origin coffee beans to add complexity to your favourite food recipes and apply your new know-how to the exhilarating world of coffee cocktails.

The possibilities are limitless with just a few skills under your belt.

WHAT IS
COLD BREW
COFFEE?

You may be accustomed to cold coffee, but let's be clear: not all cold coffee is cold brew. We all know iced coffee, hugely popular over the past decade and perpetuated by the high street chains, who deliver it in vast receptacles filled with sugar, cream and syrups – this is categorically NOT cold brew. Iced coffee starts out as hot coffee, pulled on the espresso machine and then shaken with ice, basically a chilled version of your favourite espresso-based drink. When we talk about cold brew, we're specifically referring to coffee that has been brewed with cold water – this creates a different drink entirely.

The origins of cold brew can be traced to Japan, where it is known as Kyoto-style coffee, named after its popularity in the city. The Japanese have been making cold brew since the 1600s. It was here that the brew methods evolved, from the relatively basic immersion using a toddy, to the tall and elegant cold drip towers you may see in speciality cafés today.

It is thought that the idea might actually have been developed by the Dutch, who introduced it to Japan. The theory goes that they were using the technique to transport coffee from Indonesia; the "coffee essence" could be heated and drunk after it arrived at its destination. What's interesting is that immersion-style cold brew is thought to have been invented for those with a sensitive stomach, as it has a much lower acidity than hot brewed coffee.

It's only relatively recently that cold brew arrived in the US, again with the immersion method and developing into drip methods as it emerged that a different drink could be achieved in this way. It's taken longer for Europeans to embrace it as a modern brew method.

The cold brew market is currently booming, due in part to its popularity with the younger generation who prefer the milder flavour compared to regular coffee. For the same reasons, it's also appealing to a new, health-conscious demographic – the natural low acidity and mild sweetness inherent in cold brew coffee means that it can be drunk without the dairy and sugar required to neutralize the bitterness of regular coffee. Like it or not, the "clean-eating" ethos sells and cold brew is ticking many "healthy" boxes.

And as the cold brew trend gains traction, we're starting to see more pre-packed and on-tap products aimed at mainstream audiences, with nitro cold brew the latest hot new thing, so to speak. This is cold brew charged with nitrogen, pulled from a bar tap, so that it cascades into the glass with a head like a thick stout beer and a similarly smooth and creamy texture.

WHAT ARE
THE BENEFITS?

By this point, I suspect you're almost sold on the idea of cold brew coffee, teetering on the brink of indecision before taking the plunge. Well, let me make the choice irrefutable for you.

You're probably thinking "why bother with cold brew coffee?" I mean, is your hot morning beverage not good enough or on-trend enough any more? Are you going to be made to feel like an outcast if your cup of Joe isn't served in a jam jar, in true hipster style?

Well, no, that's not the case at all; there's far more to the current popularity of cold brew than its ephemeral, hipster credentials might have you believe. First let's talk about the more scientific effects of cold brew as opposed to your regular hot brew coffee.

Coffee, not surprisingly, is more soluble at a higher temperature; essentially coffee dissolves most rapidly into its brewing water at 90.5–96°C (195–205°F). To counteract the slower brewing effects of using cold water, cold brew is brewed for much, much longer in order to increase the contact time between water and coffee grounds.

This longer, heat-free brewing method results in much-reduced levels of acidity in the finished drink. So health-wise, you'll make your dentist and doctor pretty pleased with you by protecting your tooth enamel and not aggravating your stomach.

The downside – there always is one – is that it's hard to bring out the full range of flavour notes, particularly the acidic ones, in the coffee using the cold brew method. This is not necessarily a negative – the enjoyment of those more acidic notes in coffee is a matter of personal preference – but it's a common reason why many real coffee connoisseurs are not fans of cold brew.

Though to counter this, consider that the naturally mellow and smooth notes of cold brew mean that it's rare to feel the need to turn to dairy or unhealthy sweeteners to compensate for an unbalanced drink.

Claims that cold brew is lower in caffeine than traditional hot coffee are much harder to confirm – in fact, many claim that it is higher in caffeine (showing just how much confusion there can be over the subject). In truth, you'll find this is a common theme when talking about coffee, due to a number of different variables.

In theory, cold water will extract fewer of the oils and compounds found in coffee, caffeine included, hence the argument that cold brew is a lower-caffeine drink. However, this has to be weighed up against the longer brewing time, which gives the caffeine longer to be extracted. Add to this the variation in caffeine extraction as a result of different-sized coffee grounds, and you can see why the picture is a murky one.

Another benefit of cold brew coffee, one that's a little harder to categorize, is the fact that it's a new way of drinking coffee, untainted by our existing routines and preconceptions of how coffee should be drunk.

Mind-set is a funny thing, as is the power of association. Of course, any coffee can be drunk at any time of the day, but so many of us continue to link it to our morning rituals. Cold brew, simply speaking, comes with very few of these connotations – in fact, I'd almost put it in a category of its own, so dissimilar is it to the traditional notions of coffee; it's a truly modern beverage.

In a similar vein, because there are fewer social expectations, cold brew can be taken at face value, discounting any existing preferences that you've already developed for more traditional coffee drinks. You may always drink a flat white, for example – but you suddenly find you are able to drink cold brew straight up, with no additions, allowing you to taste the flavour of the bean.

A healthier beverage, tasty and a potential game changer: that's got to be a win, right?

WHY MAKE IT
AT HOME?

Why bother to make cold brew coffee at home, you might wonder? Why, when you can wander down to your local and pick up a bottle made by a pro, when every other café has refrigerators groaning with the stuff?

The beauty of making cold brew at home is that, once you get the hang of it, you can always have a batch to hand, and you'll find that you never want your refrigerator to be without it again. It will quickly become part of your kitchen repertoire: add hot water to cold coffee concentrate to make a speedy morning brew; add a dash to your breakfast mushrooms for an interesting depth of flavour; a refreshing glass of chilled coffee over ice is just the pick-me-up for the afternoon slump; and why not finish the day on a decadent note with a cold-coffee-enhanced cocktail, without having to brew up a fresh batch?

Not only will you benefit from the convenience and personal preference, but think of the money you'll save once you've got your own routine going. By all means spend money on the things that matter, like fresh, quality beans and a decent grinder, but why put money in the pockets of faceless brands when you can do it yourself?

On top of this, bear in mind that, in the complex world of coffee, flavour is key. As flavour is a highly subjective creature, being able to understand how to tweak a recipe to your liking gives you ultimate control over your end beverage. Why buy a generic bottle from an unknown brand, or even leave it up to a barista who doesn't know your palate, when you can create your own perfect, caffeinated nectar, extracted just the way you like it and served to your personal taste?

Finally, and this is a good one, just consider the sense of achievement and wellbeing of mastering a new skill. Your ability to make friends and influence people will be at an all-time high – you'll be the hero of both sweltering summer days and the golden cocktail hour.

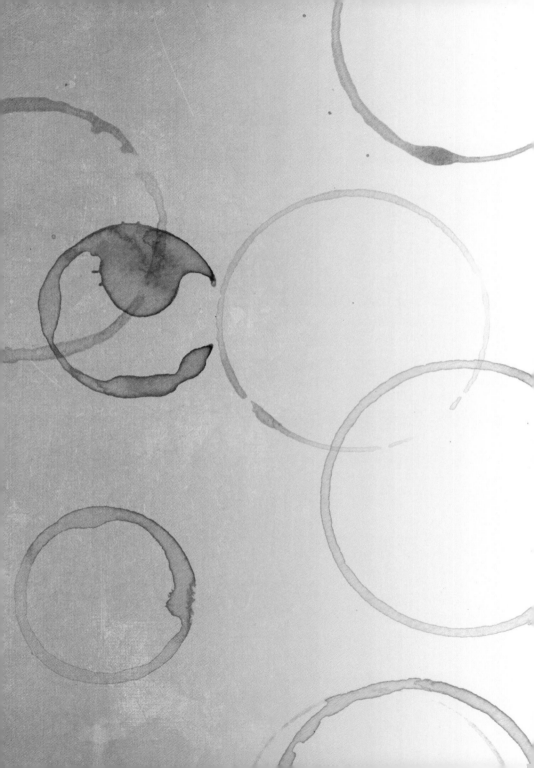

HOW TO
MAKE IT AT
HOME

So you've made the decision to make cold brew coffee at home. Good on you, it's the right one. But this being coffee, it's not the only decision you will have to make – the wonderful world of coffee is notorious for its geekery, precision brewing techniques, extraction measuring devices, high-tech equipment and many, varied thoughts on all of the above. Yes, we're essentially talking toys and brew methods here.

It's important that the brew method you choose fits into your lifestyle. You won't maintain your newly found cold brew habit if you buy equipment that just doesn't do it for you. If you invest in a cold drip tower based purely on its visual appeal but have neither the time nor patience to master it or fit it into your daily routine, then it will become little more than an expensive ornament. Vice versa, if you're someone who gets off on detail and visual dreamworks, then a simple DIY dump-it-and-leave-it immersion brew is never going to get you all hot under the collar.

And neither of the previous methods are going to work for someone who thrives on instant gratification or those who simply leave everything until the last minute. Don't worry, I'm not judging: the Japanese-style ice method was practically designed for you guys.

Of course, it's not just the practical element you need to consider: each brew method will impart its own characteristics into your coffee. If you choose a particular type of coffee because of its bright complexity, then it's unlikely that an immersion brew method will do it justice. On the other hand, if you buy a coffee that is a little unbalanced, then the immersion method could be just right to smooth out some of the spiky flavours and mellow out any negative acidity.

The short answer is that there's no simple formula to tell you which brew methods suit which coffees best. Ultimately it's a case of trial and error, but also balancing a brew method to fit your lifestyle with achieving the flavour characteristics you prefer.

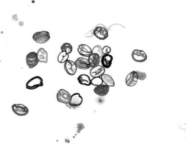

THE
COLD DRIP
METHOD

The cold drip method is probably what springs to mind when you think "cold brew". There's a very good reason for this – the cold drip towers that adorn fancy café countertops are curious looking, impressively mesmerizing and at the same time elaborately complicated, seemingly designed to confuse and blind you with theatrics.

Although there are a number of styles and brands of drip tower available, they all work on the same principle – cold water is placed in a top chamber and left to drip slowly through a flow restrictor, drop by drop on to the ground coffee below, then passes through a paper or cloth filter into a final chamber in the base of the unit.

The process relies on gravity to pull the water through the coffee grounds, slowly extracting the oils and flavours as it goes. Although contact time with the ground coffee is longer than in hot brew methods, it's nowhere near as long as in the immersion method (see page 26). The whole process takes 3–8 hours and relies on a little monitoring to ensure it's working correctly. Depending on the model you have, you may or may not be able to control the drip rate.

Because of the relatively short contact time with the ground beans, and the fact that the coffee is being filtered as it's produced, the resulting cold brew tends to be cleaner tasting, lighter in body and sometimes almost tea-like compared to other methods. The purely cold water brewing method means that acidity and bitterness are low.

This method is perfect for those who like a gentle brew and those who fancy themselves as a bit of a scientist.

HOW TO DO IT

A cold drip coffee tower is essential here. Because the water dripping needs to be controlled, this method is not something you can manage with a regular coffee brewer. If you don't have a cold drip brewer, use the immersion method on page 26 to make your cold brew instead.

How much coffee you use depends on the size of your cold drip tower, but the general rule of thumb for coffee brewing is to use 60–70g (2¼–2½oz) of coffee for every 1 litre (34fl oz) of water. So, for example, if you want to brew 500ml (18fl oz) of coffee, you'd need 30–35g (1–1¼oz) of coffee beans.

Weigh your beans, then grind them just before you brew to maintain freshness. Start with a medium to coarse grind; you can always adjust this later to perfect your brew.

Place the ground coffee in the middle chamber of the tower, above the paper or cloth filter. Some cold drip towers will allow you to add an additional paper filter above the ground coffee, to help distribute the water drips evenly across the bed of coffee.

Next measure the cold water into the top chamber, then, if you can, set the drip rate to around 1 drop every 2 seconds. You can now leave the apparatus to do its thing, but check from time to time to make sure the water is flowing through nice and evenly.

If you find your coffee is too weak or a little sour, you can grind the beans more finely to increase extraction. Conversely, if it's too intense, you can grind the beans more coarsely. You can also play around with your coffee dose: you may find you need a higher coffee-to-water ratio with some beans.

THE
IMMERSION
METHOD

Although it's not polite to draw attention to looks, the immersion method is definitely the ugly duckling of the group when it comes to cold coffee. While the cold drip method is full-on glamour, with its fancy apparatus and elegant dripping, immersion can quite literally be achieved in a bucket. Of course, there are many smarter receptacles available to purchase, but more pertinently, immersion can be done practically anywhere with a few items scavenged from around the home or, for those particularly brave brewers, the office.

This is probably the most common form of cold brewing and the results of immersion are predominantly what you'll be looking at when you see bottles, branded and spruced up, abundantly lining the shelves of cafés across town.

Coffee grounds are literally just steeped, or immersed, in cold water over a number of hours, usually 6–24. The coffee is then filtered with paper or cloth to remove some of the sediment. The bonus here is that you can simply set it up and leave it for the full brew time.

Due to the potentially much lengthier extraction time, this method tends to achieve a coffee with a heavier, more syrupy mouthfeel and toned down, often more homogeneous flavour profile. Some of the heaviness can be filtered out, but you run the danger of removing some of the flavour with it. Again, as with cold drip, acidity and bitterness are reduced in this brewing method.

There's some controversy over the ideal brewing time for the immersion method, with talk of longer brew times, anything over six hours, over-extracting the coffee to the detriment of the end brew. As with all such matters, I would suggest playing around with both the grind size and the brewing time until you get a result that you, personally, are happy with.

This brewing method is suited to those who like a brew with a bit more oomph and those who want a simple life.

HOW TO DO IT

The beauty of the immersion method is that it can be done in practically any receptacle with very little effort. Start off with a similar amount of coffee as in the drip method, so around 60–70g (2¼–2½oz) of coffee for every 1 litre (34fl oz) of water.

Weigh the coffee beans, then grind them fairly coarsely. The exact grind size should vary depending on your intended brewing time: a shorter brew time will require a finer grind, but if you intend to brew the coffee for a full 24 hours, grind the beans coarsely, otherwise you will end up with a very strong and over-extracted brew.

Put the coffee into your container and add the measured cold water.

Cover and leave the coffee mixture to steep for 6–24 hours, according to your preference. When you're happy with the concentration, pour the cold brew into a jug through a sieve to collect the majority of the coffee grounds.

Next you need to filter out the heavier sediment. Place a pour-over coffee brewer, for example a V60 with a paper filter, over a jug or jar and pour your cold brew through. This can be done a number of times, but be aware that you'll be removing body as you do this.

If you want to bring out a little more acidity from your coffee beans, you can kick-start the cold brew process with a hot water bloom. This just means that you can pour around 100ml (3½fl oz) of water, just off the boil, on to the ground coffee. You'll notice the coffee expand as carbon dioxide is released, and as it does so, a whole load of aromatics will also be released. After about 1 minute, follow with the balance of cold water and leave to steep as previously described.

If you intend to serve your cold brew over ice, be aware that the ice will dilute the coffee, so you will need to increase your coffee-to-water ratio to counteract this (see page 34).

THE
JAPANESE-STYLE
ICE METHOD

Okay, so strictly speaking this isn't a cold brewing method, as it uses hot water for the first step. However, we're including it here as it gives a completely different flavour profile, one that's typically favoured by those who really want to bring out the flavour of their beans. It also offers another great option and brew method for your growing repertoire.

The method for brewing over ice is very similar to that of regular hot drip coffee: hot water is poured over coffee grounds in a paper filter set in a Hario V60, Kalita Wave or similar pour-over device. The main difference is that the resulting coffee drips on to a bed of ice in the bottom of the container. That ice immediately cools the hot coffee, diluting it to the intended final brew ratio and, at the same time, capturing the aromatics and flavours quickly as it cools.

The hot water allows a regular extraction of coffee flavour compounds while the fast chilling traps the aromatics in situ. What this means is that you get all the bright acidity and sweetness of a regular pour-over coffee but in the form of a chilled coffee, in record time. One of the beauties of this method is that it satisfies those who really enjoy the ritual of making coffee. Note that, due to the initial hot brew, the resulting coffee is not low in acidity.

This method suits those who are after instant gratification and a bright and complex coffee.

HOW TO DO IT

The Japanese-style ice method is very similar to making a regular hot pour-over filter brew. Place a pour-over-style coffee brewer over a clean jar or container, or use a Chemex coffee maker if you have one. Insert a paper filter, rinse the filter with hot water and then discard this water.

Weigh out the beans, working to the usual ratio of 60–70g (2¼–2½oz) of beans for every 1 litre (34fl oz) of water. For 500ml (18fl oz) of coffee, you'd need 30–35g (1–1¼oz) of coffee beans and 500ml (18fl oz) of water. However, in this method a little under half the water needs to be replaced with ice, so weigh out 200g (7oz) of ice and place in the container below the coffee filter.

Grind 60–70g (2¼–2½oz) of beans to a regular filter coffee size and place in the paper filter. Fill and boil a kettle. Once it comes to the boil, let it sit for a moment so that the water is no longer boiling.

Measure out 300ml (10fl oz) of the hot water and pour a little of it over the coffee grounds, just enough to saturate the coffee bed, then leave for the water and coffee mixture to spread across the paper filter, for around 30–45 seconds.

Pour in the remaining water, slowly and in concentric circles, then allow the coffee to drip through. Wait until all the ice has melted before serving.

THE
CONCENTRATE
METHOD

First up, we're going to have to own up and admit that cold brew coffee concentrate is actually made in exactly the same way as cold brew immersion coffee. The difference is simply the ratio of water to coffee.

We're putting it here because it's a recipe you will want to nail for your ultimate portfolio of mixed cold brew beverages. Once you're happy that you've perfected your dream concentrate, you'll find it's an absolutely invaluable ingredient to have, well worth its place on the shelves of your refrigerator.

As the name suggests, the flavour characteristics are simply concentrated versions of the immersion method, so that's low acidity and mellow, syrupy sweetness with a bit of body and punch. Depending on the concentration, it can almost be used in place of an espresso for situations where it needs to punch through milk or cream, and you can make a morning americano with no need to wake up first – just add hot water to your concentrate.

Because of its low volume and high punch factor, it's a great ingredient for food and cocktail recipes; you won't need to recalibrate everything due to added fluid levels.

This method produces the perfect cold brew for experimental, aspiring chefs, as well as those who struggle with the technicalities of brewing equipment before they're fully awake.

HOW TO DO IT

So, your coffee concentrate is essentially made using the same method as the immersion brew, just more concentrated. (The clue's in the name there.) Although this time you want a coffee-to-water ratio of around 1:8. For example, that's 60g (2¼oz) of coffee to 480ml (17fl oz) of water.

From this point, the method is the same as for immersion, so grind your beans on a fairly coarse setting. Place the ground coffee into your container of choice and add the measured cold water. Cover and leave to steep for 6–24 hours.

When you're happy with the result, pour the cold brew into a jug through a sieve to collect the majority of the coffee grounds and then through a paper filter before storing in the refrigerator.

The concentrate can then be diluted with an equal quantity of hot water to make a super-speedy americano, or alternatively used as an ingredient in many food and cocktail recipes.

CASCARA

I'm going to make a wild, sweeping assumption here and presume that cascara is not an ingredient you usually keep in the kitchen cupboard. It's possible many of you will never even have come across it on your ventures into the world of coffee. If not, that's a shame, as cascara is, in fact, a very interesting and versatile ingredient.

So what is it? Coffee beans are actually the seeds found inside the fruit from the coffee tree, and that fruit is referred to as a coffee cherry. The cherry is usually discarded as a by-product of the coffee drying process, but it can be rescued, and when it is, it's usually dried – in this form, it's known as cascara. Not every roaster will have cascara available, but it's worth asking around.

Although, like coffee beans, cascara varies according to the variety of coffee and its origins, its predominant flavour is closer to tea when it is brewed, often with raisin and citrus notes. Generally, an immersion method is used to brew it cold and, as with coffee, it makes an excellent concentrate.

People cannot live on coffee alone (no, really) and cascara makes a great alternative to its darker sibling. A refreshing cold drink in its own right, it's a great palate cleanser and lends a curious note to cocktails and food recipes – I would also wager that dinner party guests won't guess the "mystery" ingredient. I think it makes a great sherry pairing, and is delicious in desserts in place of Earl Grey tea.

A word of caution: it may be a great alternative to coffee, but that doesn't mean it's caffeine-free, far from it in fact.

Cascara is great for flummoxing friends and family, and makes an interesting alternative to the dark stuff.

HOW TO DO IT

Cold brew cascara is very similar to a tea infusion and is simplicity itself – in fact, the most difficult thing is getting hold of the cascara in the first place, as you may need to order it from an online supplier. From there onward, you're on easy street.

All you need to do is weigh around 60g (2¼oz) of cascara and place in a container. Pour over 500ml (18fl oz) of cold water and leave to steep for 12–24 hours. Finally, simply strain and serve over ice.

If you want to make a cold brew cascara concentrate for use in food and cocktail recipes, simply reduce the amount of water by half. And for an edgier twist, you could try brewing a boozy version. Add a handful of cascara to a bottle of gin, vodka or bourbon and leave to infuse overnight before straining for an interesting twist on some of your favourite drinks.

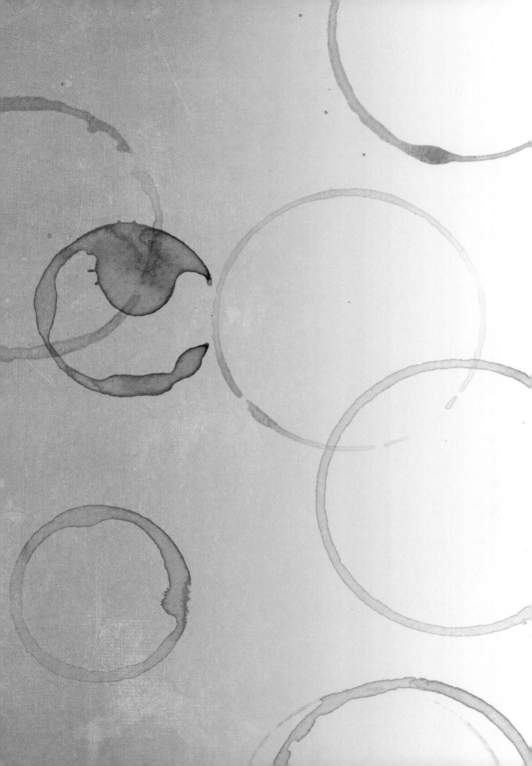

TIPS & ESSENTIAL KNOW-HOW

Right. So assuming you've made it this far, you will have mastered your chosen cold brew method(s), and with your newfound sense of accomplishment, feeling invincible, you're now ready to face the next challenge.

In this next section, you're going to learn how to get your head around the many elements involved in the process of perfecting your own cold brew. Thought it was going to be as easy as simply understanding the logistics of the various brew methods? Well, if you really want to get the best results, think again.

If you're a dab hand at brewing hot filter coffee, then you'll understand the importance of each and every element of the brewing process. If not, what follows may come as quite a surprise. Bear with me though, as once you enter this rabbit hole of new information, you'll quickly become hooked.

Let's, for the sake of argument, presume that you're feeling stoked with your cold brew, you've made something that tastes pretty darn good and you reckon you can get a fairly consistent result every time. But damn – next time you make a batch, you can't quite figure out why it doesn't taste the same. You don't think you've done anything differently… and yet.

Understanding the effect of each of the ingredients and processes involved in making cold brew is the key, not just to consistency, but to being able to deviate from the given formula and knowing how to put a personal stamp on your brew.

We all love the taste of coffee – you wouldn't be reading this otherwise – but what if you could choose a different flavour profile by buying beans from a variety of countries? Not just that, but once you've tried coffees from lots of different regions, and you start to identify the flavour notes that you like and dislike, you'll quickly begin to understand how to dial up or down certain flavour characteristics. You might want to add body to a thin coffee, tone down a particularly bright and acidic bag of beans or enhance rather than flatten complexity in a particularly interesting one.

This section will give you the confidence to do just that. It will also equip you with the tools to really drill down a decent and consistent cold brew.

STORING YOUR
COLD BREW

You might want to reconsider your refrigerator right now. Previously a space for storing perishable food items, by the time you've finished this book, you may have a better use for it...

Yes, if you hadn't guessed already, one of the beauties of cold brew coffee is that it can be stored for up to a week in a sterilized, airtight container in the chilled environment of your refrigerator. For those of you who are slaves to brewing on demand, it's going to be a potential game changer – your own cold brewed coffee on hand instantaneously.

COFFEE
ORIGINS

On the whole, most people expect coffee to taste like coffee. That might sound blindingly obvious until you taste your first coffee that, well, doesn't quite. If you're used to drinking in high street chains, then you'll be used to tasting coffee that has been roasted beyond the point where you can identify any unique characteristics from the bean itself. In the speciality world, coffee is roasted much more lightly, so that you can taste the flavour of the bean itself rather than simply the process of roasting.

It's an oft-used comparison, but it is a parallel that can be easily understood across different genres. Coffee is similar to wine in that the plant, or vine, is a product of its terroir. The soil, the altitude at which it grows, the weather conditions – all these things are unique to that precise part of the world where it grows, influencing its development and flavour perhaps more than the variety of coffee, and imparting it with characteristics in a way that transcends any one single influence.

It's probably important to note here that when you see "single origin" on a menu or bag of coffee, it simply means that it's exclusively from one region rather than a blend.

Another important thing to consider is seasonality – I've mentioned that coffee is the seed from a fruit and as such it's harvested at different times of year in the respective growing regions. So bear in mind that if you want to get the best from a particular origin, you should be buying from a fresh crop; old crop is going to taste stale in comparison. But it's here that your friendly coffee roaster or local café should be able to help you to understand this and guide you in the right direction.

The following is a list of some of the main coffee-producing regions (there are plenty more, but you know, baby steps) and what you might expect to taste from each, bearing in mind that coffee is a natural product, a fruit, and in nature there are many anomalies, with no hard-and-fast rules.

When you taste your first coffee that tastes not simply of generic "coffee" but of fruits, nuts and spices, trust me, it will all start to click into place.

ETHIOPIA

It makes sense to start in Ethiopia, since this is where Arabica, the speciality strain of the coffee plant, originated. Africa on the whole is regarded as an excellent producing environment, with many coffees from the continent considered among the best in the world. Ethiopian beans are a firm favourite with many and for good reason. They are famous for their light and complex characteristics, often honeyed floral notes, tea and bergamot flavours and crisp acidity.

When brewing Ethiopian coffees, it would be a shame to mute the elegant and complex notes, so I'd recommend trying the Japanese-style ice brewing method for starters.

KENYA

Kenya is another region famed for its quality beans, particularly noted for their juicy, fruit-driven characteristics and high acidity. Look out for lots of berry fruits, like blackcurrants, and don't be surprised if there's a hint of savoury tomato in there too.

Coffees from this region also typically lend themselves to the Japanese-style ice method, but try cold drip too, as the acidity levels in Kenyan coffee are certainly a match for this brew method.

It's worth noting here, since we're talking African coffees, that Rwandan coffee has had a bad rep in recent years due to "potato defect" – a blight that, as its name suggests, can taint a whole batch of beans with the aroma of rotten potato (nice!). However, Rwandan coffees really are well worth exploring because, when they taste good, they are truly delicious: fresh, sweet and fruity tasting, high in acidity and with some pleasing floral notes.

CENTRAL AMERICA

Coffees from Guatemala and Honduras tend to be very well balanced, with nice levels of acidity that are counteracted by a mellowness. There are also chocolate and fruit notes that make them truly versatile coffees. They would be perfect candidates for either drip or immersion brew methods.

COLOMBIA

Colombian coffees are highly versatile, with a mellow acidity and pleasing notes of caramel and nuts.

These beans would lend themselves to any of the brew methods depending on what effect you would like to achieve – use the immersion method for a beautifully balanced, mellow but fuller body with plenty of sweetness; try cold drip for a cleaner and more elegant finish; or the Japanese-style ice method to bring out the complexity and acidity. Colombian coffees would also make an excellent concentrate.

BRAZIL

While Brazil exports a lot of everyday "commodity" coffee, it's often overlooked by the speciality industry – but that's not to say that it doesn't produce some excellent beans. In fact, Brazil's naturally processed coffees are possibly more notable and far cleaner tasting than you'd expect: deliciously pronounced yet typically coffee flavours are found here, but with plenty of chocolate and nuts and a little spice.

Coffees from this region would be excellent for making a concentrate or a regular immersion brew.

PANAMA

Okay, I wasn't going to mention the coffee unicorn but... the Geisha varietal from Panama has become somewhat of a mythical beast in the coffee world. I'm not going to tell you it's better than any other region – I'll let you try for yourself – but it's famed for its supremely elegant characteristics, including juicy stone fruits and bright acidity, honey, jasmine and bergamot.

This is definitely one for the Japanese-style ice brew method.

BUYING
QUALITY BEANS

It might appear blindingly obvious, but if you buy inferior ingredients, you're never going to achieve the cold brew of your dreams.

No matter how much research you carry out on coffee origins, selecting your preferred flavour profile and deciding on your favoured brew method for each coffee, if your raw materials don't match the quality intended, your end product is never going to hit the heights that it could. Imagine making a sandwich with burned bread and mouldy cheese – you just wouldn't, right? So, in the same vein, if the roaster you buy your beans from roasts incompetently – too light, too dark or inconsistently – then you can kiss goodbye to any sense of consistency or control within your own brew.

One of the most important things you can do at this stage is to try beans. Lots of beans. Different beans, from both different roasters and different origins around the world. Not only that, but delve a little deeper and try various bean drying processes too – you might prefer the clean flavours of a washed process, but I bet there's a few of you who will love the funky, fruity sweetness of a natural process (think strawberry milkshake).

Try them all and try them lots before you pick a favourite, and then do it all again next time. This isn't a marriage, and after all, coffee is seasonal, so it's likely that the bean you fell in love with last time won't be around next.

It's worth mentioning at this point that I would always recommend Arabica beans, rather than the more common Robusta variety that you'll find in instant and "commodity" coffee, and that can give your cold brew the taste of burned rubber if they're particularly bad. I wouldn't touch them with a barge pole...

The most valuable lesson at this stage is to try as much as possible to understand what it is that you like (and what you don't). And if you're lucky enough to have one nearby, try to develop a relationship with a coffee roaster or a café you can trust. Even if you're unsure of your own palate at first, if you find the right café or roaster, they'll happily help and guide you.

WATER

We've already talked about the importance of using good-quality raw ingredients. This one might come as a shock to some of you, but water is not necessarily as clean as you might think it is, especially if it comes straight from the tap, and especially if you are living in a large city.

Why are we talking about water when all you want to do is make cold coffee? Well, it's because up to 98% of your finished drink is made up of H_2O, so it really does make a difference.

Water around the country, around the world, varies enormously in mineral content and in hardness. As such, if you were to make coffee with exactly the same beans, from the same roaster, ground and brewed in exactly the same way BUT with waters from two different sources, you would be forgiven for mistaking them for two very different drinks – such is the difference in taste.

Mind-blowing stuff. We could go on to discuss carbonate, general hardness and the very best minerals to extract the optimum flavour compounds from your chosen beans (a ratio of magnesium and calcium, since you ask), but perhaps we'll keep it relatively simple for now.

SO, WHAT ARE YOUR WATER OPTIONS?

If you were a hardcore coffee geek, you'd probably want to go all-out and use a reverse osmosis system to strip your water of mineral entirely, before dosing in your perfect mineral composition. However, let's, for argument's sake, assume you're not going for that option.

At the very least, you should be filtering your tap water with a basic jug-style water filter. Although this won't do anything to change the make-up of the water and your mineral content will remain as high, or low, as it started, it will neutralize any negative odours and flavours. This won't cure all the ailments of poor water, but it'll certainly help from a flavour point of view.

If we ignore, for a moment, issues of sustainability, then your best bet is to buy bottled water. The most widely available brands are generally pretty decent options for cold brewing – though to be absolutely sure, a good rule of thumb is to look at the label to check something called the dry residue value at 180%. You're looking for a TDS (total dissolved solids) level of around 80–120 and a fairly neutral pH level, so around 7. This should all be listed on the side of the bottle and will ensure your brew is top quality.

But you do have to factor in the environmental aspects, and even if you recycle, plastic bottles are no friends of the planet. Although you may be cutting down on plastic use by making your own cold brew, buying bottled water will easily negate this.

Your third option is perhaps the most difficult, and depends entirely on the warmth of your relationship with a local café barista. If you have a local neighborhood coffee shop that makes really good coffee, chances are they have a high-tech filtration system installed somewhere out of sight – and they *might* allow you to bring along a bottle to fill up with their water. A word of caution here – only attempt this if you're on good terms and actually frequent the café as a regular customer, and ask nicely or you may well find yourself out on the kerb pretty quickly!

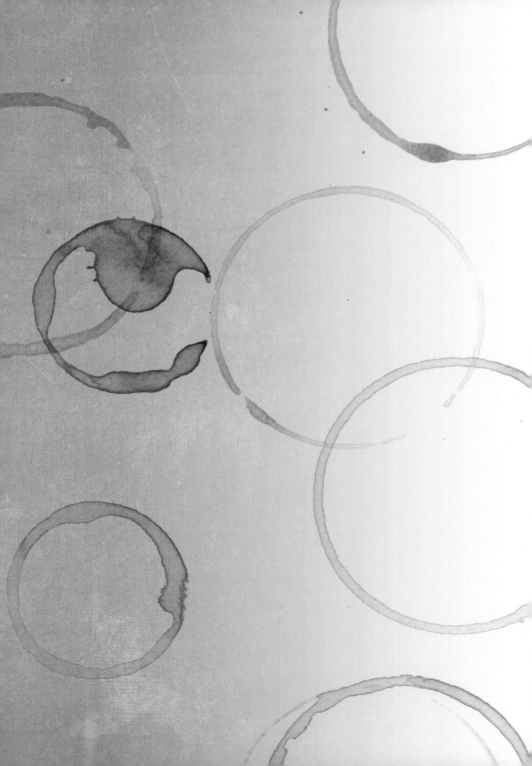

RECIPES

So, you're now a master of your domain, coffee Jedi level attained, and there are bottles of various cold caffeinated concoctions nestled on the shelves of your refrigerator.

The beauty of cold brew coffee, just in case we haven't pushed the point hard enough, is that once you have a routine going, you're never more than a short moment away from a swift grab and pour.

Here comes the fun bit – with your cold brew making now drilled down and mastered, and a production line that would put *Breaking Bad*'s Walter White to shame, it's time to take it to the next level by incorporating your brew into a whole host of cocktails, drinks and delicious food.

Before you do – and I might sound like a broken record here, but I'm going to keep saying it – however you choose to use your cold brew, whatever recipes you intend to create from it, they will only ever be as good as the raw ingredients you use. Using the freshest, well-roasted beans will take your cold brew to another level – and this in turn will truly make your recipes sing.

I'm also going to talk briefly about water again – in a different incarnation this time, and one particularly relevant to the cocktails in this chapter: ice. Once you've gone to all the effort of making a really special cold brew, it's worth taking that final extra step and thinking of ice as an active ingredient in your drink or cocktail, not as just a cube of coldness. Stirring down a Martini? You're not just stirring to chill the drink but to add dilution – as the ice melts into the Martini it not only makes the shaker, and the drink within, nice and cool but it essentially becomes part of that drink. Therefore, if the water you use to create ice is badly affected by source minerals or old pipework, for example, you'll be transferring those negative flavours and marring your otherwise perfectly considered drink.

Consider the Negroni – a drink that starts as concentrated bitterness, and slowly loosens up and mellows out as the ice melts. Ice made with badly affected water will only taint and destroy your Negroni as you sip, so it's worth taking just a little extra time with the water when making your ice.

But on a final note, these recipes are written for you to have fun with your cold brew creations. Trust your own palate here and try lots of different ingredients to get your head around flavours and subsequent pairings, before deciding on your favourites, just as you have with your coffee beans. These recipes should be considered purely as a starting point – go forth, browse, get inspired... but ultimately, get creative!

NEGRONI

SERVES 1

Also known as the Perfect Drink, the classic negroni contains just three ingredients; no mixers, just a harmonious balance of sweet, bitter and herbal. On the one hand, I'm inclined to leave it at that (why mess with a classic?), but coffee really lends something to this cocktail. Many versions replace an ingredient with coffee, but I think that knocks the drink out of kilter. An equal measure of cold brew adds another dimension without destroying the equilibrium.

INGREDIENTS

30ml (1fl oz) gin
30ml (1fl oz) Campari
30ml (1fl oz) sweet vermouth
30ml (1fl oz) cold brew
orange zest, to garnish

METHOD

Simplicity itself, just fill a rocks glass with ice cubes, pour in all the ingredients, give a quick stir and add a twist of orange zest to garnish.

NOTE: Antica Formula vermouth works well in this drink, its richness counteracting the bitterness of the coffee. Try replacing gin with bourbon for a caffeinated twist on the boulevardier.

WHITE NEGRONI

SERVES 1

Not a true negroni, of course, although the white negroni follows similar principles of balance to the classic drink. This is much sweeter and gentler than its bitter cousin, and the cascara adds an interesting twist of complexity.

INGREDIENTS

30ml (1fl oz) gin
15ml (½fl oz) cold brew cascara concentrate
15ml (½fl oz) Martini Extra Dry
30ml (1fl oz) Suze
grapefruit zest, to garnish

METHOD

Fill a rocks glass with ice cubes, pour in all the ingredients, stir and add a twist of grapefruit zest to garnish.

WORMHOLE

SERVES 1

This cocktail was created by Ryan Perry for Houston's Black Hole Coffee House and is one you will either love or loathe; the herbal, minty, cough medicine beauty of the Amaro (a bitter herbal liqueur) is not for everyone. If it's not your thing, experiment with different styles of Amaros – there are plenty around

INGREDIENTS

45ml (1½fl oz) Fernet Branca Amaro
30ml (1fl oz) cold brew
1½ teaspoons lime juice
soda water, to top up
mint sprig, to garnish

METHOD

Pour the Amaro, cold brew and lime juice into a collins glass and add plenty of ice cubes. Top up with soda water and finish with a sprig of fresh mint.

COLD
FASHIONED

SERVES 1

The old fashioned is a bar classic, made popular recently by the TV series *Mad Men*. It's often based on bourbon, but if you can, try using a Japanese Nikka whisky for its mellow fruitiness. Either way, feel free to experiment with different whiskies and bourbons – and don't scrimp on the cherry!

INGREDIENTS

1 unrefined sugar cube
2–3 dashes of Angostura bitters
60ml (2¼fl oz) Japanese Nikka whisky or bourbon
30ml (1fl oz) cold brew
orange zest, to garnish
maraschino cherries, to garnish

METHOD

Place the sugar with the bitters and a dash of water in a rocks glass and stir until dissolved. Fill the glass with ice cubes, then pour in the whisky or bourbon and cold brew. Stir gently to combine and garnish with a twist of orange zest and a cherry, or two if you are feeling particularly generous.

NOTE: Choose a coffee with good citrus notes to make the cold brew for this drink.

GIN
CASCARA SOUR

SERVES 1

The sours are cocktails containing liquor, citrus and sugar in varying ratios. Here a super-sweet and sticky sherry (we used Pedro Ximenez) takes on the sweet component while backing up the tea-like, fruity notes of the cascara.

INGREDIENTS

50ml (2fl oz) gin
15ml (½fl oz) lemon juice
15ml (½fl oz) sweet dark sherry
15ml (½fl oz) egg white (about ½ an egg white)
15ml (½fl oz) cold brew cascara concentrate
grapefruit zest, to garnish

METHOD

Place the gin, lemon juice, sherry, egg white and cascara in a cocktail shaker and shake vigorously to combine. Add some ice cubes, then shake vigorously again to cool the mixture. Strain into a coupe glass and finish with a twist of grapefruit zest.

SAKE COFFEE
SPRITZ

SERVES 1

Mention spritz and most people think of the popular Aperol version, refreshing and yet cloyingly sweet. Here we've combined coffee with Japanese sake and sparkling wine to create a drink that's gently boozy but totally acceptable for daytime drinking. If you can't find yuzu, then grapefruit is a good alternative.

INGREDIENTS

50ml (2fl oz) sake
30ml (1fl oz) cold brew
60ml (2¼fl oz) sparkling white wine
soda water, to top up
yuzu zest, to garnish

METHOD

Fill a tall glass with ice cubes, add the sake, cold brew and sparkling wine. Top up with soda water and garnish with a twist of yuzu zest.

NOTE: Choose a coffee with zesty, floral notes to make your cold brew for this drink. Something Ethiopian would work well here.

WHITE
RUSSIAN

SERVES 1

Classically made with vodka, coffee liqueur and cream, this beverage is favoured by "the dude", of *The Big Lebowski* fame. Here we've replaced the liqueur with a coffee concentrate to punch through the creaminess and swapped vodka for a spiced, fruity rum. This is a dessert in drink form.

INGREDIENTS

60ml (2¼fl oz) spiced rum
30ml (1fl oz) cold brew concentrate
30ml (1fl oz) single cream

METHOD

Fill a rocks glass with ice cubes, add the rum and cold brew concentrate and stir to combine. Then pour over the cream so that it swirls psychedelically through the drink and serve immediately.

SAKE COFFEE
MARTINI

SERVES 1

Sake, Japanese rice wine, is having its moment in the spotlight right now. Gentle and floral with a hint of muskiness, it's an interesting substitution for vermouth in this martini. Rather than dominating, the coffee harmonizes with the floral notes of both the sake and gin for a soft twist on the classic martini.

INGREDIENTS

60ml (2¼fl oz) gin
15ml (½fl oz) sake
15ml (½fl oz) cold brew
umeboshi or a green olive, to garnish

METHOD

Fill a cocktail shaker with ice cubes and stir in the gin, sake and cold brew. Strain into a martini glass and garnish with an umeboshi or green olive for a pleasing umami finish.

NOTE: Choose a light, floral coffee for this recipe, such as an Ethiopian variety, to complement the sake. If you haven't come across them before, umeboshi are Japanese salt-preserved plums.

SHERRY-RINSED
CASCARA MARTINI

SERVES 1

A good martini is a beautiful thing; gin and a dash of vermouth, little else is needed to create the most elegant drink of cocktail hour. There is room for a number of variations though, and this one is an absolute winner. The sweetness of the cascara plays off the dry sherry in a curiously clever dance.

INGREDIENTS

60ml (2¼fl oz) gin
15ml (½fl oz) cold brew cascara concentrate
dash of fino sherry
grapefruit zest, to garnish

METHOD

Fill a cocktail shaker with ice cubes and stir in the gin and cascara to cool. Pour a dash of sherry into a frozen martini glass, swill around and then discard the sherry (if that happens to be into your mouth, we won't judge). Strain the gin and cascara into the glass and garnish with a twist of grapefruit zest.

HARD
SHAKE

SERVES 1

Milkshakes are wonderful things, but sadly most these days just don't match the standards of the classic fifties diner shake, lovingly made by expert hands. Here we've blended coffee concentrate with some mellow bourbon to bring a degree of sophistication back to this most indulgent of drinks.

INGREDIENTS

30ml (1fl oz) bourbon
30ml (1fl oz) cold brew concentrate
5 scoops of vanilla ice cream
a few dashes of chocolate bitters
dark chocolate shavings, to serve

METHOD

Place all the ingredients in a blender and blend until smooth. Pour into a sundae glass for nostalgic appeal, sprinkle the chocolate on top and keep away from the kids.

NOTE: Choose a good-quality ice cream for best results, and use chocolate with at least 70% cocoa solids.

PETIT CAFÉ

SERVES 1

We love herbaciously complex green Chartreuse and it goes surprisingly well with our favourite caffeinated beverage. This is our take on petit café, a cocktail created by H Joseph Ehrmann of Elixir in San Francisco for the 2006 Chartreuse Cocktail Competition. Imagine Irish coffee meets white Russian.

INGREDIENTS

30ml (1fl oz) green Chartreuse
50ml (2fl oz) cold brew concentrate
60ml (2¼fl oz) double cream, whipped

METHOD

Fill a cocktail shaker with ice cubes and stir in the green Chartreuse and cold brew concentrate. Strain into a wine glass and top with the whipped cream.

ESPRESSO
GIN & TONIC

SERVES 1

Here we've playfully combined a gin and tonic with the increasingly popular espresso tonic. It's a drink that allows you to flex your creative muscles, selecting your coffee and gin for the flavours and aromatics they contain. It's essentially a blank canvas for you to build on with your choice of garnish.

INGREDIENTS

30ml (1fl oz) gin
30ml (1fl oz) cold brew concentrate
tonic water, to top up
garnish of your choice

METHOD

Fill a tall glass with ice cubes, add the gin and cold brew concentrate and top up with tonic water. Get creative with your garnishes depending on the coffee that you use.

NOTE: The classic chocolate and nutty flavours of a Brazilian coffee would contrast well with a zest of lime, or a slice of mango would emphasize the aromatic notes of Ethiopian coffee. Experiment!

NAIROBI
SOUR

SERVES 1

The New York sour, created in Chicago (yes, really), dates back to the late 1870s. Here we've replaced its claret floater with a shot of fruity Kenyan coffee, which achieves a similar fruit-driven – but altogether punchier – snap.

INGREDIENTS

60ml (2¼fl oz) bourbon
30ml (1fl oz) lemon juice
15ml (½fl oz) sugar syrup (see page 86)
30ml (1fl oz) egg white (about 1 egg white)
25ml (¾fl oz) fruity Kenyan cold brew
maraschino cherry, to garnish
lemon zest, to garnish

METHOD

Place the bourbon, lemon juice, sugar syrup and egg white in a cocktail shaker and shake vigorously to combine. Add some ice cubes, then shake vigorously again to cool the mixture. Strain into a rocks glass, float the cold brew on top, then garnish with a cherry and a twist of lemon zest.

CAMPARI & COFFEE
SODA

SERVES 1

Campari, created in 1860, is a delicious yet head-twitchingly bitter aperitif. In 2006, Campari controversially changed the recipe, removing the red carmine dye, famously derived from crushed cochineal beetles. This drink is the perfect daytime libation, refreshing and arguably a whole lot classier than the omnipresent spritz, with the coffee adding another dimension of bitterness.

INGREDIENTS

60ml (2¼fl oz) Campari
30ml (1fl oz) cold brew
soda water, to top up
orange slice, to garnish

METHOD

Fill a tall glass with ice cubes and add the Campari and cold brew. Top up with soda water and garnish with a slice of orange.

MEXICAN
COFFEE

SERVES 1

Mezcal is the smoky, lesser-known sister of tequila, made in Mexico from the agave plant. It's traditionally drunk neat, but it lends itself to short cocktails exceptionally well. Here it is paired with the herbal bitter Cynar with a dash of sherry and cold brew for a seriously grown-up drink. To take it a step further, add a little smoked salt to the rim of the glass for a deliciously saline note.

INGREDIENTS

50ml (2fl oz) Mezcal
25ml (¾fl oz) Cynar
15ml (½fl oz) cold brew, preferably Mexican
15ml (½fl oz) fino sherry
3–4 dashes of Angostura bitters
orange zest, to garnish

METHOD

Fill a tall glass with ice cubes, add all the ingredients and stir. Serve garnished with a twist of orange zest.

ESPRESSO
MARTINI

SERVES 1

There's no denying that an espresso martini is a modern classic, though you might think twice about ordering one if you can't be sure of the quality of the ingredients. Perhaps the best thing about the drink is its invention in London's Soho in the 1980s. Bartender Dick Bradsell was asked by a customer to make her a drink that would "wake me up, then f*** me up". Here we've doubled up on the caffeine by adding cascara to the recipe – it should really do the trick.

INGREDIENTS

50ml (2fl oz) vodka
30ml (1fl oz) cold brew concentrate
20ml (⅝fl oz) cold brew cascara concentrate
coffee beans, to garnish

METHOD

Fill a cocktail shaker with ice cubes, add all the ingredients and shake to cool. Strain into a martini glass, float some coffee beans on top to garnish and enjoy.

COFFEE
CAIPIRINHA

SERVES 1

Caipiriniha is a cocktail synonymous with Brazil, made from the national spirit cachaça. Similar to rum, cachaça is created from fermented then distilled sugar cane juice and makes for a very potent beverage. We've upped the ante here with a shot of cold brew concentrate for a cocktail with serious punch.

INGREDIENTS

½ a lime, cut into wedges
1 teaspoon sugar
25ml (¾fl oz) cold brew concentrate
60ml (2¼fl oz) white cachaça

METHOD

Muddle the lime and sugar in a rocks glass, then add the cold brew concentrate and cachaça and stir to combine. Pack the glass with ice cubes and enjoy immediately.

COFFEE
PUNCH

SERVES ABOUT 5

The joy of punch is that it's a party drink, and the beautifully balanced bowl you start with is likely to become a very different concoction as the evening progresses and revellers top it up with whatever's to hand. But with this in your bowl at the beginning of the evening, you know you're off to a good start...

INGREDIENTS

200g (7oz) mixed berries
1–2 tablespoons sugar, to taste
300ml (10fl oz) cold brew
1 bottle of red wine
100ml (3½fl oz) sloe gin
150ml (5fl oz) whisky

METHOD

Place the berries and sugar in a large punch bowl and muddle together to crush the berries and dissolve the sugar. Add all the other ingredients and stir to combine, adjusting quantities to taste.

NOTE: Kenyan coffees with berry fruit flavours will work well here. And choose a light and fruity red wine to complement the coffee: perhaps one made with a Gamay grape.

PORTER COFFEE
COCKTAIL

SERVES 1

Beer cocktails have come into their own in recent years, popping up on many a menu. Porter, with its rich malty notes, is an obvious partner for coffee, with bourbon and sweet vermouth adding to the marriage and riffing on complexity.

INGREDIENTS

30ml (1fl oz) bourbon
60ml (2¼fl oz) cold brew
90ml (3fl oz) porter
15ml (½fl oz) sweet vermouth
2–3 dashes of chocolate bitters

METHOD

Fill a tall glass with ice cubes, pour in all the ingredients and stir to combine. Enjoy.

IRISH
COFFEE

SERVES 1

Created in the 1940s, Irish coffee is the choice drink for internal central heating. It's also the one cocktail specified as compulsory in the ultimate international barista cocktail competition – World Coffee In Good Spirits Championship – held every year. This cold version subverts these preconceptions.

INGREDIENTS

15ml (½fl oz) sugar syrup (see below)
25ml (¾fl oz) Irish Whiskey
175ml (6fl oz) cold brew
60ml (2¼fl oz) double cream

METHOD

Combine the sugar syrup and whiskey in a glass mug then stir in the cold brew. Shake the cream until thickened, then pour over the back of a spoon into the glass so that it floats. Garnish with grated chocolate, if liked.

NOTE: To make sugar syrup at home, place equal quantities by weight of sugar and water in a saucepan and heat gently, stirring, until all the sugar has dissolved. Once cooled, the syrup can be kept in a sterilized bottle in the refrigerator for up to a month.

COLD BREW COFFEE
TONIC

SERVES 1

A twist on the espresso tonic, which is proliferating in cafés across the world, this is a gentler, fruity take. Choose a citrus and soft fruit-driven coffee.

INGREDIENTS

100ml (3½fl oz) cold brew
tonic water, to top up
lemon wedge, to garnish

METHOD

Fill a tall glass with ice cubes and pour in the cold brew. Top up with tonic water and garnish with a wedge of lemon.

CASCARA BERGAMOT
& TONIC

SERVES 1

A refreshing long drink that combines the fruity, tea-like notes of cascara with fresh bergamot, a citrus fruit typically associated with Earl Grey tea, for a little trickery. Bergamot is very aromatic, so adjust the quantity of juice to taste.

INGREDIENTS

100ml (3½fl oz) cold brew cascara
tonic water, to top up
a dash of bergamot juice
bergamot zest, to garnish

METHOD

Fill a tall glass with ice cubes and add the cascara. Top up with tonic water and a squeeze of bergamot juice, then garnish with a twist of bergamot zest.

COLD BREW
ICE CREAM
FLOAT

SERVES 1

We are certainly not advising you to replace your morning beverage with one of these, or even to have one every day, but just occasionally, when the desire for a sweet and indulgent retro diner classic takes hold of you, this should hit the spot nicely. Suck it through a stripy straw for bonus retro points!

INGREDIENTS

60ml (2¼fl oz) cold brew concentrate
cream soda, to top up
1 scoop of coconut ice cream
dark chocolate shavings, to serve

METHOD

Fill a tall glass with ice cubes, add the cold brew concentrate and top up with cream soda. Place a generous scoop of coconut ice cream on top and finish with a sprinkling of dark chocolate shavings.

VIETNAMESE
ICED COFFEE

SERVES 1

Vietnamese iced coffee is traditionally brewed directly over ice, often with condensed milk in the bottom of the cup, but this version gives you the same flavour without the hassle. Known as *cà phê đá*, it's usually made with very dark beans, but you should use a well-developed and balanced roast here.

INGREDIENTS

60ml (2¼fl oz) cold brew concentrate
condensed milk, to taste

METHOD

Place some ice cubes in a tall glass and add the cold brew concentrate. Stir in condensed milk to taste; it's very sweet and rich, so you'll only need a little.

GROWN-UP
COFFEE MILK

SERVES 1

This is a simple, booze-free comfort drink for a welcome cuddle of nostalgia. You can use regular milk, or experiment with different nut milks, but I really like the classic combination of coffee and almond that we've used here.

INGREDIENTS

50ml (2fl oz) cold brew concentrate
200ml (7fl oz) almond milk

METHOD

Fill a tall glass with ice cubes and pour in the cold brew concentrate. Top up with almond milk to serve.

NOTE: For the ultimate coffee milk, choose a coffee with chocolatey, nutty notes to make your cold brew concentrate.

COFFEE
FRENCH TOAST

SERVES 2

French toast is an indulgent breakfast favourite for three good reasons: carbs, eggs and dairy. Add coffee to the mix and it's elevated to new levels. I'm a sucker for a sweet/savoury combo, so serving bacon on the side is an absolute no-brainer. Add a dash of orange liqueur to the batter if you want to up the luxury levels.

INGREDIENTS

2 eggs
100ml (3½fl oz) double cream
50ml (2fl oz) cold brew
pinch of salt
1 teaspoon finely grated orange zest
4 thick slices of brioche
knob (pat) of butter
crispy streaky bacon, to serve

METHOD

Place the eggs, cream, cold brew, salt and orange zest in a shallow bowl and whisk lightly to combine. Soak the brioche slices briefly in the mixture, turning once, until saturated but not soggy.

Heat half the butter in a heavy-based frying pan over a medium heat and add 2 slices of brioche. Cook, turning once, until the outsides are crisp and golden but the middle is still a little soft. Remove from the pan

Repeat with the remaining butter and brioche. Serve hot, topped with the streaky bacon.

SPICY COFFEE
HOLLANDAISE

SERVES 2

This is inspired by a dish on my favourite brunch menu, that of the under-the-radar Fields café on Clapham Common, London. They use espresso and spicy sriracha sauce in their hollandaise, although the exact recipe remains a secret. This is a mellower version, but feel free to mix it up. Best served over poached eggs on a bed of sautéed spinach, crispy pancetta and toasted crumpets.

INGREDIENTS

100g (3½oz) butter
2 egg yolks
50ml (2fl oz) cold brew
pinch of salt
lemon juice, to taste
Tabasco sauce, to taste

METHOD

Melt the butter gently in a saucepan over a low heat, skimming off any white scum that floats to the surface, then remove from the heat and keep warm.

Place the egg yolks, cold brew and salt in a heatproof bowl and whisk to combine. Set the bowl over a small saucepan of gently simmering water, making sure the water does not touch the bottom of the bowl. Continue to whisk the mixture until it is pale and thick.

Remove from the heat and slowly whisk in the melted butter, a little at a time, until incorporated. Add a squeeze of lemon juice and Tabasco sauce to taste.

COFFEE & HAZELNUT
COOKIES

MAKES ABOUT 15

These little biscuits are called *ricciarelli*. Hailing from Siena in Tuscany, they are traditionally made with almonds. Here the almonds are replaced with hazelnuts to complement the hint of coffee and add a richer flavour.

INGREDIENTS

150g (5½oz) blanched hazelnuts
1 large (extra-large) egg white
150g (5½oz) caster sugar

100g (3½oz) icing sugar, sifted
½ teaspoon baking powder
1 tablespoon cold brew concentrate

METHOD

Preheat the oven to 180°C (350°F), Gas Mark 4 and line a baking sheet with nonstick baking paper.

Place the hazelnuts in the bowl of a food processor and process until finely chopped, the texture of ground almonds. Whisk the egg white in a mixing bowl until it forms stiff peaks.

Place the ground hazelnuts in a separate mixing bowl with the caster sugar, icing sugar, baking powder and cold brew concentrate. Fold in the egg white to form a sticky dough. If it's too wet, add a little more icing sugar.

Shape the dough into about 15 small balls and arrange them, well spaced, on the prepared baking sheet, pushing a thumb down into the centre of each to flatten slightly.

Bake for 10–15 minutes until the edges of each cookie are starting to turn golden; the centre should still be quite soft. Transfer to a wire rack to cool. These will keep in a sealed container for 2 days.

SHERRY CASCARA
ZABAGLIONE

SERVES 4

Although it gives the arms a bit of a work out, this dessert is simplicity itself, the perfect sweet, creamy and boozy conclusion to any meal. The cascara in this recipe is curiously delicious, playing off the sherry.

INGREDIENTS

4 egg yolks
50g (1¾oz) soft light brown sugar
100ml (3½fl oz) oloroso sherry
50ml (2fl oz) cold brew cascara
biscuits or cookies, to serve

METHOD

Place the egg yolks and sugar in a large heatproof bowl. Set the bowl over a small saucepan of barely simmering water, making sure the water does not touch the bottom of the bowl. Whisk the mixture until glossy.

Turn the heat up a little, add the sherry and cascara and continue whisking until thickened and very light and fluffy. Divide between 4 small dishes and serve with little biscuits or cookies for scooping up with.

COFFEE
PANNA COTTA

SERVES 6

Coffee is the star of the show here, so it's the ideal choice to showcase the cold brew flavour. For extra points, you can try serving the panna cotta with ingredients to complement the taste of your chosen coffee bean – for example, pair a Kenyan coffee with stewed, spiced berries, or a Colombian brew with candied orange.

INGREDIENTS

1½ leaves of gelatine
350ml (12fl oz) double cream
75ml (2½fl oz) whole milk
50ml (2fl oz) cold brew concentrate
50g (1¾oz) icing sugar

METHOD

Soak the leaves of gelatine in a little cold water for 5 minutes until soft. Squeeze to remove excess water.

Meanwhile, place the remaining ingredients in a saucepan over a low heat, stirring, until the mixture just reaches simmering point. Remove from the heat, add the softened gelatine and stir gently until it has dissolved completely. Pour the mixture into 6 small moulds or ramekins and chill in the refrigerator for at least 4 hours or overnight until set. Dip the moulds briefly in warm water before turning the panna cottas out on to serving plates.

MINI COLD BREW
DOUGHNUTS

MAKES 25

Known as *zeppole*, these Italian doughnuts are traditionally made on St Joseph's Day in Sicily, but they are sold on the streets all year long. I've added cardamom, cold brew and orange zest for an aromatic take on the original.

INGREDIENTS

140g (5oz) plain flour
2 teaspoons baking powder
pinch of salt
¼ teaspoon ground cardamom
50g (1¾oz) caster sugar
1 teaspoon finely grated orange zest

50ml (2fl oz) cold brew
2 eggs
125g (4½oz) ricotta
oil, for deep-frying
icing sugar, for dusting

METHOD

Sift the flour, baking powder, salt and cardamom into a mixing bowl. Stir in the caster sugar and orange zest until well combined.

In a separate bowl beat the cold brew together with the eggs, then mix into the dry ingredients with the ricotta to form a stiff batter.

Half-fill a heavy-based saucepan or deep-fat fryer with the oil and heat to 190°C (375°F), or until a cube of bread browns in 1 minute. Drop teaspoonfuls of the mixture, 3 at a time, into the oil and cook until golden, turning once. Drain on kitchen paper, then dust with icing sugar before serving warm.

TIRAMISU

SERVES 6

How could I leave out the best known of all coffee desserts? The name translates as "pick-me-up" and how better to do that than with a dose of cold brew coffee?

INGREDIENTS

4 egg yolks
75g (2¾oz) caster sugar
150ml (5fl oz) marsala wine
350ml (12fl oz) double cream
450g (1lb) mascarpone

250g (9oz) savoiardi biscuits or sponge fingers
300ml (10fl oz) cold brew concentrate
dark chocolate, for grating

METHOD

To make the filling, whisk the yolks in a heatproof bowl until they thicken, then whisk in the sugar until fully incorporated. Add the marsala and cream, then set the bowl over a small saucepan of gently simmering water, making sure the water does not touch the bottom of the bowl. Continue to whisk the mixture until light and fluffy. Beat the mascarpone until softened, then fold into the cream mixture.

Dip the biscuits, one at a time, in the cold brew concentrate, so they are fully covered but not soggy. Use half the biscuits to line the bottom of a serving dish, then cover with half the cream. Repeat with another layer of biscuits and the remaining cream.

Grate a good layer of chocolate over the top of the tiramisu, then cover and chill in the refrigerator for at least 2 hours or overnight before serving.

COFFEE CHOCOLATE
TART

SERVES 6

Coffee and chocolate is an age-old pairing for good reason, and what better vehicle than this richly bitter and indulgent tart? Keep it classic by using a typically coffee-flavoured bean to make your cold brew concentrate, or accentuate the attributes of coffees from different origins by adding a splash of orange liqueur or zest to the filling, or perhaps a few drops of bergamot oil, some chopped fruits and/or spices, using the tart as a delectably blank canvas.

INGREDIENTS

225g (8oz) dark chocolate (at least 70% cocoa solids)
225ml (8fl oz) double cream
2 tablespoons soft light brown sugar
50g (1¾oz) butter
75ml (2½fl oz) cold brew concentrate
1 ready-made cooked shortcrust pastry case

METHOD

Break the chocolate into small pieces and place in a mixing bowl. Place the cream in a small saucepan over a medium heat until it reaches simmering point, then pour over the chocolate and set aside for 1–2 minutes.

Add the remaining ingredients to the mixing bowl and stir until the chocolate has melted and the mixture is glossy. Pour into the pastry case and allow the filling to cool and set in the refrigerator, for about 2 hours, before serving.

BOURBON
COFFEE SAUCE

SERVES 6

What could be more delicious than a bourbon-pimped salted caramel sauce? You guessed it – add an intense coffee hit for an addictive sauce that you'll want to smother on pancakes, ice cream, brownies... even yourself.

INGREDIENTS

250g (9oz) soft light brown sugar
50g (1¾oz) butter
100ml (3½fl oz) double cream
50ml (2fl oz) bourbon
50ml (2fl oz) cold brew concentrate
pinch of sea salt flakes

METHOD

Place the sugar in a nonstick saucepan over a medium heat until it starts to melt. Continue to heat, stirring occasionally, until it turns a deep amber colour, but be careful, as it can burn very quickly.

Remove from the heat and add the remaining ingredients. Return the pan to the heat and stir for another minute or so until the ingredients are fully combined and the sauce is glossy.

COLD BREW
MARINADE

MAKES 250ML (9FL OZ)

Great for adding interest to summer barbecues or warming winter dinners, a good marinade recipe is a must in anyone's repertoire. With cold brew adding a great depth of flavour, this marinade will transform steak or pork. Simply pour over chops, ribs, steaks or larger joints and leave in the refrigerator overnight before grilling or roasting the next day.

INGREDIENTS

1 tablespoon soy sauce
2 garlic cloves, crushed
100ml (3½fl oz) red wine
100ml (3½fl oz) cold brew
1 tablespoon soft light brown sugar
1 tablespoon olive oil
freshly ground black pepper

METHOD

Combine all the ingredients in a plastic bag or shallow dish, add the meat and rub all over. Seal the bag or cover the dish and leave to marinate in the refrigerator overnight.

GLOSSARY

UK	US
Baking paper	Parchment paper
Biscuits	Cookies
Caster sugar	Superfine sugar; if you don't have any, process the same quantity of granulated sugar in a food processor or blender for 1 minute
Dark chocolate	Semisweet chocolate; if the chocolate should have a high percentage of cocoa compared to sugar, such as 62–70% cocoa, it is bittersweet chocolate
Double cream	Heavy cream
Full-fat milk	Whole milk
Egg (large), Egg (extra-large)	for US egg sizes, choose a size larger than given in UK recipes – for example, a UK medium egg is a US large egg
Gelatine, leaves of	Gelatin, sheets of
Grilling	Broiling
Heavy-based frying pan	Heavy skillet
High street	Main street, where there is a concentration of stores; high street chains refer to retail chain stores typically found on Main streets and in shopping malls
Icing sugar	Confectioners' sugar, also known as powdered sugar
Jam jar	Screw-top jar
Joint (of meat)	Roast (of meat)
Jug	Pitcher; also used to refer to a liquid measuring cup
Kerb	Curb
Kitchen paper	Paper towels
Sieve	Strainer
Pastry case	Pastry shell (crust)
Plain flour	All-purpose flour
Single cream	Light cream
Soda water	Club soda
Soft brown sugar	Brown sugar
Sponge fingers	Ladyfingers
Streaky bacon	Bacon
Tap	Faucet

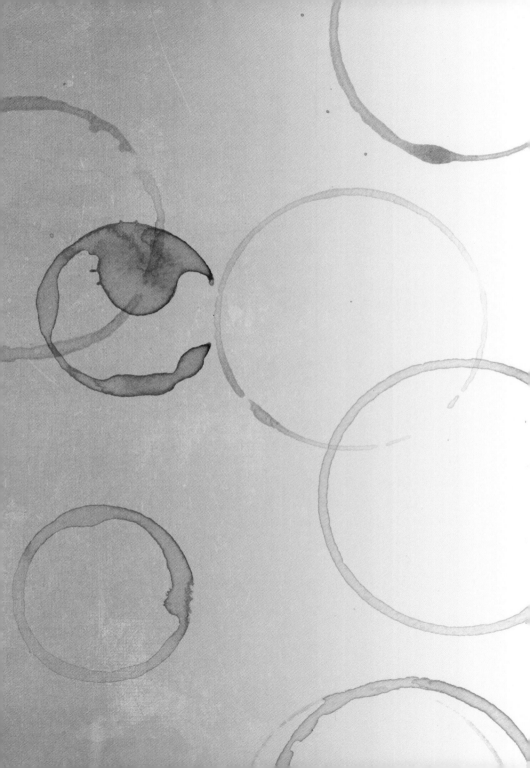

ACKNOWLEDGEMENTS

A huge thank you goes to Jamie Treby, Edd Kimber, Dave Jameson, Scott Bentley and many more for their sage advice and input on *Cold Brew Coffee*.

Thank you to all my friends and family who I neglected for a month and to Luca for helping me to celebrate.

PUBLISHER'S NOTES

Standard level spoon measurements are used in all recipes.

1 tablespoon = one 15 ml spoon
1 teaspoon = one 5 ml spoon

Both imperial and metric measurements have been given in all recipes. Use one set of measurements only and not a mixture of both.

Eggs should be medium unless otherwise stated. The Department of Health advises that eggs should not be consumed raw. This book contains dishes made with raw or lightly cooked eggs. It is prudent for more vulnerable people such as pregnant and nursing mothers, invalids, the elderly, babies and young children to avoid uncooked or lightly cooked dishes made with eggs.

Once prepared these dishes should be kept refrigerated and used promptly.

Ovens should be preheated to the specific temperature – if using a fan-assisted oven, follow manufacturer's instructions for adjusting the time and the temperature.

This book includes dishes made with nuts and nut derivatives. It is advisable for customers with known allergic reactions to nuts and nut derivatives and those who may be potentially vulnerable to these allergies, such as pregnant and nursing mothers, invalids, the elderly, babies and children, to avoid dishes made with nuts and nut oils. It is also prudent to check the labels of pre-prepared ingredients for the possible inclusion of nut derivatives.

Chloë Callow is editor of *Caffeine* magazine and is thoroughly steeped in the world of coffee. She works as an expert in water filtration for the coffee industry, and has written articles and reviews for a range of coffee and cocktail magazines and apps. She has also worked with the UK chapter of the Speciality Coffee Association of Europe.

An Hachette UK Company
www.hachette.co.uk

First published in Great Britain in 2017 by Mitchell Beazley,
an imprint of Octopus Publishing Group Ltd
Carmelite House
50 Victoria Embankment
London EC4Y 0DZ
www.octopusbooks.co.uk
www.octopusbooksusa.com

This edition published in the US in 2021

Distributed in the US by Hachette Book Group
1290 Avenue of the Americas
4th and 5th Floors
New York, NY 10104

Distributed in Canada by Canadian Manda Group
664 Annette St.
Toronto, Ontario
Canada M6S 2C8

ISBN 978 1 78472 753 6

Printed and bound in China

10 9 8 7 6 5 4 3 2 1

Commissioning editor: Joe Cottington
Senior editor: Pauline Bache
Creative director: Jonathan Christie
Designer: The Oak Studio
Illustrator: Emma Dibben
Senior production controller: Allison Gonsalves